SPHINXES AND CENTAURS

Cavendish
Square

New York

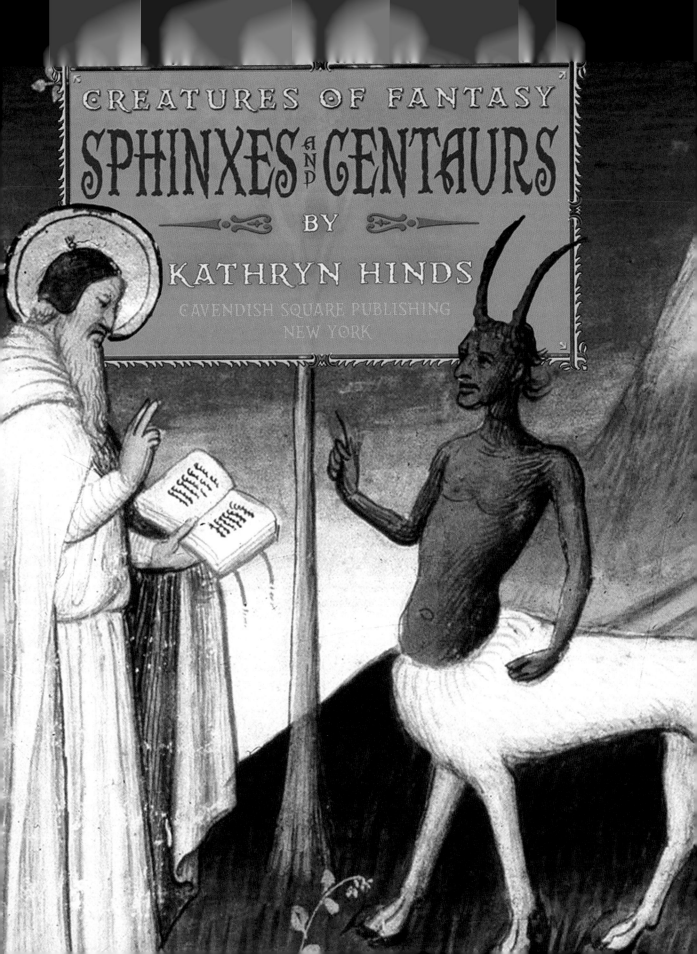

CREATURES OF FANTASY

SPHINXES AND CENTAURS

BY

KATHRYN HINDS

CAVENDISH SQUARE PUBLISHING
NEW YORK

To Owen

Published in 2014 by Cavendish Square Publishing, LLC
303 Park Avenue South, Suite 1247, New York, NY 10010

Copyright © 2014 by Cavendish Square Publishing, LLC

First Edition

LIBRARY OF CONGRESS CATALOGING-IN-PUBLICATION DATA

Hinds, Kathryn, 1962- Sphinxes and centaurs / Kathryn Hinds. p. cm.—(Creatures of fantasy) Includes bibliographical references and index. Summary: "Explores the mythical and historical backgrounds of sphinxes and centaurs, including the Buraq of Islamic tradition, the Great Sphinx of ancient Egypt, man-animals of Mesopotamia, and the Gandharvas of India"—Provided by publisher. ISBN 978-0-7614-4927-0 (hardcover)— ISBN 978-1-62712-054-8 (paperback) —ISBN 978-1-60870-683-9 (ebook) 1. Sphinxes (Mythology)—Juvenile literature. 2. Centaurs—Juvenile literature. I. Title. BL820.S66H56 2013 398'.45—dc23 2012000517

Editor: Deborah Grahame-Smith   Art Director: Anahid Hamparian   Series Designer: Michael Nelson

Photo research by Debbie Needleman. The photographs in this book are used by permission and through the courtesy of: *Front Cover:* © Réunion des Musées Nationaux/Art Resource, NY. *Back Cover:* © Photos 12/Alamy. *Page i:* The Metropolitan Museum of Art, New York, NY. U.S.A. Image copyright © The Metropolitan Museum of Art. Image source: Art Resource, NY; *pages ii-iii:* © akg-images/Newscom; *page vi:* © The Print Collector/Alamy; *page 8:* © KENNETH GARRETT/National Geographic Stock; *page 10:* © akg-images/Herbert Kraft/Newscom; *page 11:* © Hemis/Alamy; *page 12:* © Topham/The Image Works; *page 13:* © ullstein – Archiv Gerstenberg/The Image Works; *page 14:* © Eyebyte/Alamy; *page 18:* © DeA Picture Library/Art Resource, NY; *page 20:* © The Questioner of the Sphinx, 1863 (oil on canvas). Vedder, Elihu (1836-1923)/Museum of Fine Arts, Boston, Massachusetts, USA/Bequest of Mrs. Martin Brimmer/The Bridgeman Library; *pages 22, 33:* © Gianni Dagli Orti/The Art Archive at Art Resource, NY; *page 25:* © Erich Lessing/Art Resource, NY; *page 27:* © Mary Evans Picture Library/The Image Works; *page 29:* © The Granger Collection, New York; *page 30:* © Peter Horree/Alamy; *page 32:* © The Natural History Museum, London, UK/The Image Works; *page 35:* © Mary Evans Picture Library/Alamy; *page 36:* © Charles Walker/Topham/The Image Works; *page 38:* Royal Library of the Netherlands, KB, KA 16 Folio 66r; *page 39:* © Alinari/Art Resource, NY; *page 40:* © Constellation of the Zodiac: Sagittarius, the Archer from Ta'lim dar ma'rifat i taqvuim, 1498. Abu Ja'far al-Tabari/The Trustees of the Chester Beatty Library, Dublin/The Bridgeman Art Library/Getty Images; *page 43:* © Rubin Museum of Art/Art Resource, NY; *pages 44, 52:* © Réunion des Musées Nationaux/Art Resource, NY; *page 47:* MS Hunter 229 f.6r Sagittarius from the Hunterian Psalter (vellum). English School (12th century)/© Glasgow University Library, Scotland/The Bridgeman Art Library; *page 49:* Wedding of Peirithous & Hippodameia. Catalogue Number: London F272, British Museum, London, United Kingdom; *page 51:* Female Centaur and Companion Making Music. Neopolitan School (gouache), Italian School (19th century). Phillips, The International Fine Art Auctioneers, UK/Photo © Bonhams, London, UK/The Bridgeman Art Library; *page 54:* © bilwissedition Ltd & Co. KG/Alamy; *page 55:* Sweet, piercing sweet was the music of Pan's pipe, illustration from "The Story of Greece" by Mary Macgregor, 1st edition, 1913 (colour print). Crane, Walter (1845-1915)/Private Collection/The Stapleton Collection/The Bridgeman Art Library; *page 56:* © 2003 Charles Walker/Topfoto/The Image Works.

Printed in the United States of America

front cover: A centaur out hunting with his dog, portrayed on a plaque from twelfth-century France.
back cover: A satyr—part man and part goat—in the 2005 film *The Lion, the Witch, and the Wardrobe*.
half-title: This four-inch-long sphinx was carved out of ivory in Mesopotamia more than 2,700 years ago.
title page: A painting in a French book from 1375 depicts a legend about a satyr asking the hermit Saint Anthony to pray for all the fauns, satyrs, and other mythic creatures of the wilderness.

CONTENTS

Le   *Cynocefale*

A cynocephalus, one of the dog-headed people said to live in tribes in Africa and India. Stories of this creature probably arose from early travelers' attempts to describe baboons. In fact, *cynocephalus* now forms part of the scientific name of some baboon species.

INTRODUCTION

In the CREATURES OF FANTASY series we celebrate the deeds of dragons, unicorns, and their kin. These fabulous beasts have inhabited the imagination and arts since the beginnings of human history, immortalized in paintings and sculptures, mythology and literature, movies and video games. Today's blockbuster fantasy novels and films—*The Chronicles of Narnia, Harry Potter, Lord of the Rings, Eragon,* and others—have brought new popularity to the denizens of folklore, myth, and legend. It seems that these creatures of the imagination have always been with us and, in one way or another, always will be.

Belief in the fantastic, in wonders, appears to be a lasting part of the human experience. Even if we no longer believe that dragons and unicorns actually exist, we still like to think about what the world might be like if they did. We dream and daydream about them. We make up stories. And as we share those dreams, read and tell those stories, we not only stir our imaginations, but also explore some of the deepest hopes and fears of humanity. The power of the dragon, the purity of the unicorn, the wildness of the centaur, the mystery of the sphinx, the allure of the mermaid— these and more are all part of our human heritage, the legends of our ancestors still alive for us today.

COMBINATION CREATURES

Myriad kinds of mortal creatures were brought forth,
endowed with all sorts of shapes, wondrous to behold.

~EMPEDOCLES, FIFTH CENTURY BCE

SPHINXES, CENTAURS, AND SIMILAR CREATURES are hybrid beings—that is, they are part one thing and part another. In them, human and animal meet. Sometimes it is the best of both worlds, sometimes the worst. Sometimes the combined human and animal features add up to an essence that goes beyond both, that may even be divine. Whether they have been seen as gods, monsters, or something else, combination creatures have intrigued people since prehistoric times.

HUNTERS AND HUNTED

Imagine yourself living tens of thousands of years ago. Humans are few, far outnumbered by animals. Some of the animals are good to eat; others would be happy to eat you. Either way, they

Opposite: When an artist carved this lion-human hybrid out of the tusk of a woolly mammoth 30,000 years ago, cave lions were the mightiest predators around. Seven feet long and four feet tall at the shoulder, they lived throughout Ice Age Europe and Asia, competing with humans for reindeer and other game.

are powerful influences on your existence, representing both life and death. Certain animals may also embody specific qualities, such as strength, bravery, swiftness, or abundance. The animals are part of your world, and you are part of theirs. The connection between you and the animals may go even deeper: in some ways, you are part of each other.

The important place of animals in prehistoric societies shows up in cave paintings and other art, much of which was probably

part of religious or ceremonial practices. This art includes images of hybrid beings, such as a 30,000-year-old ivory sculpture of a human with a lion's head. Perhaps the most famous prehistoric hybrid being, nicknamed the Sorcerer of Les Trois-Frères, was carved and painted more than 10,000 years ago on a cave wall in France. The Sorcerer appears to be a dancing man with a shaggy coat and an antlered head. Was he a shaman dressed in the skin of a deer? Was he a god or some other kind of spirit? All we can know for sure is that the artist who painted him believed there was something fascinating and powerful about the combination of animal and human characteristics.

A drawing published in the 1920s shows the Sorcerer of Les Trois-Frères in detail. The original figure is thirteen feet above the ground in a hard-to-reach section of the cave, with hundreds of small, overlapping images of horses, bison, and reindeer beneath him.

DIVINE HYBRIDS

More than five thousand years ago, the ancient Egyptians began depicting many of their deities as animal-headed humans. The god of mummies and burials, Anubis, had the head of a jackal or wild dog. Thoth, god of wisdom, writing, and the moon, had the

head of an ibis (a kind of bird). Crocodile-headed Sobek was a god of water, protection, and strength. The head of Khepri, a god of renewal and the rising sun, took the form of a scarab beetle. The sky god Horus and the sun god Re (or Ra) were falcon headed. Re's daughter Hathor, sky goddess and protector of women, had the head or ears of a cow. When she was angry, she turned into the fierce lioness-headed goddess Sekhmet. Cat-headed Bast, on the other hand, was a gentle goddess of music, joy, and motherhood.

This is just a small selection of the deities worshiped in ancient Egypt. Most of them could alter their forms, from part human to fully human—or to fully animal. Some had more than one animal form. Thoth, for example, could be pictured as a baboon as well as an ibis.

An Egyptian tomb painting from around 1,600 years ago features the animal-headed god Anubis tending the mummy of the deceased.

Part-animal deities have also been honored in India since ancient times. One of the most popular is Ganesha, who has the head of an elephant. A cheerful god who loves learning, literature, and sweets, he is often called the Remover of Obstacles, and it is traditional to pray to him for help in overcoming problems. Another beloved figure is the god Hanuman, who has a human body but a monkey's face and tail. He is renowned for marvelous feats of strength, such as lifting up and transporting an entire mountain, and even more honored for his courage, patience, and unfailing assistance and devotion to the hero Rama, one of the forms taken by the god Vishnu.

The monkey god Hanuman lifts up a mountain covered with healing herbs to go to the aid of a wounded hero. When people call on Hanuman to help them in times of trouble, they often pray, "Victory to thy thunderbolt strength."

One of India's major deities, Vishnu has long been worshiped as the preserver of creation. Constantly working for the good of the world, he has appeared on the earth in different forms during times of crisis. Long, long ago he took a tortoise or part-tortoise shape, known as Kurma, to retrieve the nectar of immortality from beneath the ocean. Later, to defeat a terrible demon, he became Varaha, a man with a boar's head. In another case he manifested as a lion-man, Narasimha, in order to rid India of a cruel king. Vishnu's trusty mount Garuda hates wickedness as much as he does. With a man's body and the beak and wings of an eagle, Garuda flies Vishnu from place to place to defeat evil wherever it may be found.

The Prophet's Steed

Scriptures and myths of religions from around the world tell of special mounts that carried deities, prophets, and other important figures on their spiritual journeys. According to Islamic tradition, the Prophet Muhammad once rode upon an amazing creature called the Buraq. Its body was horselike, but it had a human head, an eagle's wings, and a peacock's tail. The Buraq—whose name means "lightning"—could understand all human languages, and its breath smelled like the most wonderful perfume.

The Buraq seems to have belonged to the angel Gabriel. Muhammad told a group of his helpers that one night Gabriel appeared to him, and then "a white animal which was smaller than a mule and bigger than a donkey was brought to me." When Muhammad first tried to get onto the Buraq, it bucked and kicked. Gabriel scolded it, saying that no one who had ever ridden it was dearer to God than Muhammad was. Ashamed of itself, the Buraq settled down and let Muhammad mount.

Vishnu and his wife, Lakshmi, goddess of good luck and prosperity, riding the divine man-eagle Garuda.

This was the beginning of an amazing journey, as Muhammad recounted: "The animal's step (was so wide that it) reached the farthest point within the reach of the animal's sight. I was carried on it, and Gabriel set out with me till we reached the nearest heaven." With Gabriel and the Buraq, Muhammad visited seven heavens in all, where he met and talked with Jesus, Moses, Abraham, and other great men of God. Then the Buraq carried him to Jerusalem before returning him to his home in Mecca. All this happened in a single, miraculous night, thanks to the lightning swiftness of the Buraq.

THE EGYPTIAN SPHINX

In front of these pyramids is the Sphinx, a still more wondrous
object of art, but one upon which silence has been observed,
as it is looked upon as a divinity by the people of the neighbourhood.

~PLINY THE ELDER, FIRST CENTURY

THE BIRTHPLACE OF THE SPHINX, OR HUMAN-headed lion, is not entirely certain. Some evidence suggests it was known in Asia Minor (modern Turkey) as much as five thousand years ago. But not too long after that, the sphinx showed up in Egypt, where it thrived so well that it's hard not to think of ancient Egypt as the creature's homeland.

Carved in stone, Egyptian sphinxes guarded tombs, temples, and palaces. The lion body probably symbolized animal strength; the human head showed that this raw power was controlled by intelligence. With the faces of godlike kings, and sometimes queens, sphinxes were not only powerful protectors but also emblems of the might and wisdom of Egypt's rulers. People who saw the sphinxes were filled with awe—especially in the presence of the greatest sphinx of all.

Opposite: The Great Sphinx of Giza is one of the world's most famous—and dramatic—images of an animal-human hybrid.

15

The Great Sphinx

On the plain of Giza in the Egyptian desert, not far from the edge of the fertile green land along the Nile River, the Great Sphinx crouches. Towering above it are the three Great Pyramids, regarded since ancient times as Wonders of the World. These remarkable structures were built as tombs for kings who ruled Egypt roughly 4,500 years ago. The Sphinx was sculpted during the same period. The Great Pyramids and the Sphinx were part of a large cemetery complex, which included seven smaller pyramids and a large number of other tombs. In ancient times there were also several temples in the cemetery. At least one of these temples had its own sphinx statues—four of them, each about 26 feet long.

The Great Sphinx was nine times bigger. At close to 70 feet tall and 240 feet long, it is probably the world's largest monument carved from a single piece of stone. And its creation may have been begun almost by accident. Many archaeologists think that when workers were building Giza's pyramids and temples, some of the stone they used was quarried from the area around the Sphinx. Eventually they got down to a layer of rock that wasn't really good building material. Then someone noticed something: the stone they'd removed had left a rectangular mound that looked sort of like a lion's body. Why not take advantage of the shape and carve it into a sphinx?

Of course, it is possible that the Sphinx was a planned element of the cemetery all along. In any case, it became an important part of the complex, with a temple of its own situated just beyond its front paws. Unfortunately, the carvings on that temple were destroyed in ancient times, and no writings survive from the pyramid age to explain the Great Sphinx's original meaning and purpose. This is one of the things that has made the colossal creature seem so mysterious.

Yet there are clues that might help us understand the Sphinx better. The Pyramids and the Sphinx are on the west bank of the Nile, since the ancient Egyptians believed that the realm of the dead lay to the west, where the sun sets. The Sphinx, however, faces the east, the direction of the rising sun and the land of the living. So the Sphinx could be there to guard the land of the dead from living people (especially ones who might turn out to be tomb robbers). Or, perhaps the Sphinx's purpose is to form some kind of link between the living and the dead. There are a number of possible solutions to the mystery of the Sphinx's purpose, and more than one of them might be true—the ancient Egyptians were happy to embrace a broad range of beliefs, often all at the same time.

Rediscovery

Around four thousand years ago, the Giza cemetery fell out of use and people stopped tending to its monuments. Over the decades and centuries, sand blown by the desert winds covered up more and more of the Sphinx, until its lower body was completely buried. Then one day, more than a thousand years after the colossal sculpture was carved, an Egyptian prince got tired during a hunting trip near the Pyramids:

He relaxed in the shadow of this great god [the Sphinx] and sleep overcame him just at the time that the sun was at its height. Then he discovered the Majesty of this Great God was speaking out of his very own mouth, just as a father addresses his son, saying, "Look at me, gaze at me, my own son. . . . My state is that of one in trouble . . . and the desert sand is covering the place in which I sit. I have waited to have you carry out that which is in my heart for I know you, saying, 'You are my son and my protector.'"

A portrait of Thutmose IV on the wall of his tomb.

The prince's dream convinced him to have the sand cleared away from the Sphinx. This deed proved him worthy to become king of Egypt, and from 1400 to 1390 BCE he ruled as Thutmose IV. How do we know about his dream and its meaning? After taking the throne, Thutmose recorded the whole story on a stone plaque set up between the Sphinx's paws.

Because of other plaques dedicated to the Great Sphinx, we also know that during this period the ancient Egyptians began to regard it as an image of the god Hor-em-akhet, meaning "Horus of the Horizon." A modern author explains that Hor-em-akhet was believed "to guard the gates of the beyond, the gates through which the day star appears each morning and disappears each evening." The worship of the Great Sphinx as Hor-em-akhet continued for roughly 1,500 years.

Then Christianity, followed by Islam, came to Egypt. The old gods were mostly forgotten, the ancient monuments were neglected, and sand once more began to cover the Sphinx. When French forces under Napoléon Bonaparte landed in Egypt in 1798, the Great Sphinx was visible only from the neck up. In the following century there were various attempts to clear away all the sand, but no one succeeded until the twentieth century. It took a French engineer and his team eleven years, and in 1936 the Sphinx was at last completely freed, to awe and mystify people once more.

More Lion-Bodied Beings

The Sphinx of Giza was one of the very first sphinxes to be portrayed in ancient Egyptian art, but a great many more followed. Nearly all of them, like the Great Sphinx, wore a head cloth called a *nemes*, with a rearing snake on the front of it. This was a traditional headdress for Egyptian kings, and the sphinxes often wore a crown on top of the *nemes*.

Clearly, sphinxes were identified with the king or royal power in some way. And in ancient Egypt, royal power was also divine power, since the ruler was regarded as a child of the gods and became a god himself after death. The king also had the divine responsibility of keeping the forces of order and disorder in balance for the good of all Egypt, and this cosmic balance was probably another thing that the sphinx symbolized.

At first sphinxes were always portrayed crouching, wingless, and with men's faces. As time went on, variations developed. Sphinxes appeared standing up, often stomping on Egypt's enemies. Some sphinxes gained wings, although they usually kept them folded at their sides. For a time in one northern Egyptian city, sphinxes

Over the centuries, the Great Sphinx became mostly buried in sand—which may have made it seem even more mysterious, as in this 1863 painting showing a man waiting for the ancient figure to whisper words of wisdom to him.

had male faces surround by lions' manes. And when Hatshepsut became one of Egypt's handful of female rulers, she had sphinxes carved with her own face. A few kings' wives, too, were portrayed as sphinxes. In one famous image, a queen named Tiy is shown as a woman-headed lion attacking female enemy prisoners.

There were also sphinxes that did not have human heads. The two most common creatures like this were the hieracosphinx, with a falcon's head, and the criosphinx, with a ram's head. The criosphinx became especially important as a symbol of Amon, who was regarded as king of the gods for several hundred years. The

avenue leading to Amon's main temple was lined with impressive sculptures of ram-headed lions.

In addition to sphinxes carved in stone, there were numerous smaller images. For example, around four thousand years ago a person was buried with a little golden sphinx. The owner of this amulet probably hoped to be protected by the royal power symbolized by the sphinx. On the journey to the afterlife, it could never hurt to have a god-king on your side.

MAN-ANIMALS OF MESOPOTAMIA

Beasts of the mountains and the seas,
which I had fashioned out of white limestone and alabaster,
I had set up in [the] gates.

~ASHURNASIRPAL II, NINTH CENTURY BCE

ABOUT THE SAME TIME THE GREAT SPHINX was made, the people of Mesopotamia (today's Iraq) were carving sphinxes into small stone cylinders that were used to press images into clay. As Mesopotamian empires fell and new ones arose, the sphinxes of the region grew larger and larger. They also developed a look all their own.

Mighty Guardians

The human-headed lions of Mesopotamia are usually known as Lamassu. But Lamassu were not always lion bodied: a great many of them had the bodies of bulls. Both animal forms were extremely powerful, and both lion and bull Lamassu had large, outspread eagle wings and wore tall, flat-topped, cylinder-shaped crowns.

Opposite: This Lamassu, standing almost fourteen feet high, guarded a doorway in a Mesopotamian palace during the 700s BCE.

23

Sometimes a Lamassu had a woman's head, but usually it was male. Typically a Lamassu's face was that of a dignified man with a long, curled beard.

Although images of these creatures were often used to decorate furniture and other objects, they also had a much more important function. Thanks to their combination of animal strength, human intelligence, and the divine gift of flight, Lamassu were powerful protectors. They were especially good at guarding entryways—the gates of cities and palaces, the doors of houses and rooms. Lamassu were often carved on tablets of clay or stone that were buried under doorways. Since it was believed that every day Lamassu held open the gates of dawn for the sun god, it is not surprising that people thought they'd be handy around the entrances of human structures, too.

In 879 BCE Ashurnasirpal II, ruler of Assyria (an empire based in northern Mesopotamia), held a huge celebration to dedicate his new capital. Its splendid palaces, temples, and office buildings were located at the city's highest point. Ashurnasirpal described his home with pride: "I built thereon [a palace with] halls of cedar, cypress, juniper, boxwood, teak . . . as my royal dwelling and for the enduring leisure of my lordship. . . . I made [the palace] fittingly imposing." To protect all this magnificence from evil influences, the king made sure to have pairs of Lamassu stationed at important entryways.

One palace room was guarded by two 5-foot-high crouching female Lamassu. Most impressive, though, were some of the male Lamassu. More than 10 feet tall, they were cleverly sculpted with five legs. This way, if you saw one from the front, it appeared to be standing still and alert—but if you saw the Lamassu from the side,

it seemed to be striding forward. Ashurnasirpal's successors for the next two hundred years followed his example by protecting their palaces with monumental five-legged Lamassu, which sometimes reached a height of over 14 feet. Rulers in neighboring lands, from Asia Minor to Persia, also adopted the Lamassu for their own palaces and temples.

MONSTERS AND EVIL SPIRITS

Mesopotamian myths and legends were full of part-human, part-animal beings. Some were friends to gods and humans, but others were not. For example, there was the demon Lamashtu, imagined as having a woman's body, lion's head, donkey's teeth, and bird's talons. She would enter a pregnant woman's house at night and try to touch the woman's belly. If she managed to do so seven times, the unborn baby would die.

Lamashtu could be fended off by the image of another demon, Pazuzu. He was generally portrayed with a somewhat doglike face, and his chest might be covered with scales. He usually had the wings and talons of a bird, but sometimes had lion's claws instead of talons. Pazuzu, like many Mesopotamian demons, could use his energies both to help and to harm. One statue of him was

Ashurnasirpal II, holding in his right hand the special kind of sickle that the gods of Assyria often used to kill monsters.

carved with these words: "I am Pazuzu, king of evil spirits, and of the winds that come raging down from the mountains." These winds were often thought to carry disease, and they were also associated with sandstorms. But if you could get Pazuzu on your side, he was a powerful ally.

Pazuzu may have been related to another bird-man, called Anzu or just Zu. Anzu, a bearded man who was an eagle from the chest down (although sometimes he was shown as a lion-headed eagle), was a demon or spirit of storms. He was supposed to serve the sky god Enlil, but one day he stole the god's powerful Tablet of Destiny and hid it on a mountaintop. Belet-ili, Mistress of All Gods, sent her son Ninurta to go after Anzu and retrieve the tablet. In another version of the myth, it was not Ninurta but the god Marduk who defeated the treacherous Anzu.

Heroes and Hybrids

Marduk was the hero of the epic *Enuma Elish*, written by the Babylonians of Mesopotamia sometime before 1100 BCE. In the climax of this mythological poem, Marduk overcomes the sea goddess Tiamat, who has created a number of monsters to assist her in a war between the older gods and the younger gods. Among her creatures are several human-animal hybrids: "a scorpion-man, . . . a fish-man, and a bull-man / Bearing merciless weapons, fearless in battle." As we have already seen, bull-men were monsters that could be beneficial to humans. As for fish-men, one of the region's oldest gods, Ea, was in fact part man and part fish.*

Even scorpion-men sometimes had a helpful aspect. An archer with a scorpion's body from the waist down and a man's body

*For more on human-fish creatures, see *Mermaids*, another book in this series.

from the waist up was portrayed on a boundary stone from ancient Babylon. Probably he was thought of as a protector for the property marked by the stone, scaring off would-be trespassers.

In a painting based on ancient Babylonian images, Marduk battles the goddess Tiamat, who has taken on a dragon-like form.

Scorpion-men could definitely be frightening. *The Epic of Gilgamesh*, whose fullest existing version was written down in the 600s BCE, tells how the brave warrior-king Gilgamesh encountered two scorpion-people, a male and female:

> Trembling terror they inspire, the sight of them is death,
> their frightening aura sweeps over the mountains.
> At the rising and setting they watch over the Sun.
> When Gilgamesh saw them, trembling terror blanketed
>   his face.

Luckily, the scorpion beings realized that Gilgamesh, who had more than one divine ancestor, was only one-third human. So instead of killing him right away, they asked him why he was traveling in such a dangerous region. Once satisfied with his answer, they allowed him to pass, and Gilgamesh continued on his journey in search of the secret of eternal life.

The Manticore

Just east of Mesopotamia lay Persia (modern Iran), which had its own set of fantastic creatures. Among them was a strange beast called the manticore. Its name comes from the Old Persian word *martikhoras*, which meant "man killer." First-century Roman author Pliny the Elder, drawing on the work of an earlier Greek writer who had spent time in Persia, gave the classic description of the manticore: "Along with the face and ears of a man, it has a triple row of teeth that fit together like the teeth of a comb, blue-grey eyes, a lion's body the colour of blood, and it uses its tail to sting like a scorpion. Its voice falls between the sound of pan-pipes and trumpets, it is fleet-footed, and has a particular taste for human flesh." By Pliny's time, the manticore was said to live in Ethiopia. In the modern era, there have been rumors of manticores in the jungles of Indonesia. The Indonesian manticore supposedly needs only a single bite or scratch to kill its victim, who dies instantly. The manticore then devours every bit of the prey, leaving not even a single bone uneaten.

Above: A manticore, as pictured in a book from the 1500s.

THE GREEK SPHINX

Farther on we come to the mountain from which they say the Sphinx,
chanting a riddle, sallied to bring death upon those she caught.

~Pausanias, second century

BY ABOUT 1500 BCE, SPHINXES WERE APPEARING in the art of many places around the eastern Mediterranean Sea. It took until the 700s BCE, though, for sphinxes to show up in Greece. These Greek sphinxes always had wings and were nearly always female. They were often depicted in carvings on grave markers and were thought to protect the dead. Sculptures from one Greek city showed the creatures carrying warriors off the battle-field, perhaps escorting their spirits to the afterlife. Sphinxes were also portrayed in statues atop temple columns, as well as in vase paintings and as decorations on other objects. But while sphinxes in art might be attractive and helpful, the Sphinx of Greek myth and literature was quite different.

Opposite: This six-foot-high sphinx once graced the top of a column at the temple where a priestess known as the Oracle of Delphi delivered mysterious prophecies from the Greek god Apollo.

The Riddler of Thebes

The city of Thebes was in trouble. Because of a terrible crime committed by a former ruler, which the people had let him get away with, the gods had decided to punish the Thebans. This was a job for a monster, and so the gods summoned the Sphinx from her home in Ethiopia.

It was said that the Sphinx was the daughter or granddaughter of Echidna, the mother of all monsters. Echidna was half woman and half snake; her daughter Chimera—the Sphinx's other possible mother—had three heads and was part lion, part goat, and part snake. With such a parent, the Sphinx seems to have been born to master the art of terrorizing people. In addition, the Muses (goddesses of poetry and other arts) gave her a special weapon to use in Thebes: a riddle.

A modern artist's concept of Chimera, who was either the mother or sister of the Sphinx of Thebes.

The Sphinx settled down on a mountain outside the city. From there she would unpredictably swoop down on people and demand they answer her riddle. The price for a wrong answer was death—and not a pleasant one, because first the Sphinx strangled her victims, then she ate them.

Many people met this fate, including the son of King Creon. Creon and his people were growing desperate to end the Sphinx's reign of terror. At last the king sent out a plea for help. In a play from around 410 BCE, the Greek poet Euripides has Creon's widowed sister, Jocasta, explain:

When the Sphinx bore down our city with her raids,
my husband gone, Creon proclaimed my marriage:
whoever might guess the clever maiden's riddle,
to him I should be wed.

Along came a mysterious stranger, Oedipus. The Sphinx confronted him, but he was not afraid. He calmly listened to her riddle: "What being with one voice has sometimes two feet, sometimes three, sometimes four, and is weakest when it has the most?" Then, as clever as he was brave, he calmly gave his answer: "A human being, who crawls on all fours as an infant, walks on two legs in the prime of life, and leans on a staff in old age."

Oedipus was right. By solving the riddle, he freed Thebes from the Sphinx for good. Some versions of the story say she threw herself off

An ancient Greek vase painting shows Oedipus (the beardless young man holding the spear) giving his answer to the Sphinx's riddle.

a cliff, enraged at her defeat. Other versions say that after winning the Sphinx's battle of wits, Oedipus killed her. In any case, he did go on to marry Jocasta and soon afterward became king of Thebes.

Since ancient Greek times, the story of Oedipus and the Sphinx has been retold in many ways. In Ralph Waldo Emerson's 1841 poem "The Sphinx," the riddling creature has grown old and weary, despairing that she will ever find a truly wise human. When finally a traveler comes along who is able to answer her question, she is overwhelmed with joy:

Uprose the merry Sphinx,
And crouched no more in stone;
She melted into purple cloud,
She silvered in the moon.

TERROR ON THE WING

The Sphinx was not the only winged female hybrid creature who plagued humans in Greek mythology. Older even than the gods were the Furies, terrifying-looking women with red eyes, dog heads, bat wings, and snakes instead of hair. It was the Furies' job to pursue and punish those who committed violence against family members. They followed their prey without rest, lashing them with whips, until the criminals died or went insane. Sometimes the Furies were assisted by bird-women called Harpies.

The ancient Greek poet Hesiod described the Harpies as beings with "lovely hair, who in the speed of their wings keep pace with the blowing winds, or birds in flight." They sound rather pleasant, don't they? Their name, however, comes from an ancient Greek verb meaning "to snatch" or "to seize." In the words of one modern author, originally "they were wind-spirits that carried off anyone whom the gods wished to cause to disappear." Since images of Harpies were sometimes carved or painted on tombs, they, like sphinxes, also seem to have played a role in carrying souls to the realm of the dead.

In ancient literature, Harpies were portrayed as disgusting, greedy creatures who loved to dive out of the sky and stretch out their talons to grab away people's meals. The traveling hero Jason visited a king named Phineus who had been driven to starvation by the Harpies, who always watched his food. Phineus told Jason,

"They immediately all swoop down like the black cloud of a whirling tornado. . . . They ravage and sweep away my feast, and pollute and upset the cups." Luckily, Jason had two of the North Wind's sons with him. They flew up to do battle with the Harpies and succeeded in driving them away from Phineus's land to a remote island.

Later, the hero Aeneas and his companions arrived on this very island. Having been tossed about on a stormy sea for days after fleeing the conquered city of Troy, they were exhausted, depressed, and starving. Luckily, there were plenty of goats and cattle on the island, so they slaughtered some and prepared a feast. Unluckily, these animals belonged to the Harpies, who showed up in a rage. In the *Aeneid*, an epic by the Roman poet Virgil, Aeneas says:

> No monster is more terrible than the Harpies, no plague, no wrath of the gods more dire. . . . They are birds with the faces of young girls. Disgusting filth comes from their stomachs; their hands have claws and they are always pale from hunger. . . . Suddenly, with a fearful swoop from the mountains they are upon us, and with a loud clang they flap their wings, plunder the feast, making every dish filthy with their dirty hands; with the foul stench comes a hideous scream.

An illustration of a Harpy, complete with the "lovely hair" described by Hesiod, from a 1652 book titled *A Natural History of Birds*.

Aeneas and his men fought the Harpies, but not very successfully. The battle ended with the Harpies' leader laying a curse on them: "Famine shall fasten upon you, in return for trying to kill us." Indeed, Aeneas would undergo many more hardships before he finally found a new homeland for himself and his companions.

5

CENTAURS

He had indeed to struggle with beings who were gods
on their mother's side, who possessed the swiftness of horses,
who had the strength of two bodies, and enjoyed in addition
the experience and wisdom of men.

~DIODORUS SICULUS, FIRST CENTURY BCE

THE CENTAUR IS A HUMAN FROM THE WAIST up and a horse from the waist down. Unlike such creatures as the Sphinx and the Harpies, it is usually male. Ancient Greek authors often called centaurs beast-men, "a wild folk," and similar names. Some of the earliest writers may actually have thought of the centaurs simply as some tribe of rowdy barbarians, and not specifically as part-horse beings. Such hybrids had been depicted in Greek art, however, since around 725 BCE.

Related creatures also showed up in art from time to time. All of them had human heads, arms, and chests, but the bucentaur was a bull from the waist down, while an onocentaur was donkey bodied. An ichthyocentaur was a fish below the waist, but with a horse's front legs. So when writing about human-horse hybrids,

Opposite:
The constellation Sagittarius (The Archer) commemorated the centaur Chiron, the great hunter and wise teacher of a number of Greek gods and heroes.

A fierce-looking onocentaur, armed with a club.

the ancient Greeks and Romans sometimes called them hippocentaurs (*hippo* was Greek for "horse"), to make it perfectly clear what they were talking about.

Origins

The poet Pindar, who lived in the fifth century BCE, seems to have been the first writer who described centaurs specifically as half human and half horse. He also gave the earliest description of their origin. It all began with Ixion, king of a people called the Lapiths.

Ixion had come before the gods to be judged for a crime. The king of the gods, Zeus, granted him forgiveness. But then Ixion fell in love with Hera, Zeus's wife, and followed her to her room. There he thought he was with Hera, but in fact it was Nephele, a cloud maiden Zeus had created in Hera's exact image. Zeus, seeing that Ixion was betraying the gods' hospitality and could never be trusted, condemned him to terrible punishment in the underworld.

Meanwhile, Nephele was pregnant. The gods seem to have completely abandoned her—she was only a cloud, after all—and alone in the wilderness, she gave birth to "her babe of monstrous breed, who had no honour amongst men nor in the laws of heaven." Pindar's story ends: "And she reared him up, and called him by the name of Centaurus, who consorted with the Magnesian mares . . . and thence there came into being a host wondrous to look upon, resembling both their parents, the dam's side down, the upper side the sire's."

As with most myths, there were other versions of the story. Some people, according to the third-century writer Philostratus, "used to think that the race of Kentauroi (Centaurs) sprang from trees or rocks." Three centuries before Philostratus, though, the Roman statesman and philosopher Cicero had decided the real origin of the centaurs was in the human mind: "Who [in this day and age] believes that the Hippocentaurus or the Chimaera ever existed? . . . The years obliterate the inventions of the imagination, but confirm the judgements of nature."

Cicero, as pictured by fifteenth-century artist Joos Van Ghent.

The First Horsemen

Around the same time as Cicero, the historian Diodorus Siculus recorded that some people were saying the offspring of Nephele were called hippocentaurs "because they were the first to essay [attempt] the riding of horses, and that they were then made into a fictitious myth, to the effect that they were of double form." This is similar to a popular modern theory that the mythical centaurs were based on the inventors of horseback riding—nomads from the great plains of Asia. Greeks first came into contact with one of these nomad peoples, the Scythians, in the eighth century BCE.

Although the Greeks at this time had horses they used for pulling chariots, they were not familiar with riding. Scythians, on the

other hand, probably started learning to ride even before they began to walk. By the time they were adults, they were completely at ease on horseback. They sat on little more than a saddlecloth and hardly needed reins, generally riding with their hands free (the better to shoot their powerful bows). Scythians also tended to sit forward on the horse, right behind its neck.

To people who had never before seen anyone astride a horse, these Scythian riders must have appeared to be completely joined to their mounts, especially from a distance. It would have taken only a bit of misunderstanding, exaggeration, or imagination to come up with the idea of beings who were half horse and half human. In addition, the Greeks regarded the Scythians as barbarians: uncivilized, wild, and warlike—qualities that were also typical of the Greek image of the centaur.

An illustration of Sagittarius from a 1498 Arabic book shows a centaur with the type of bow used by Central Asian nomads, who were highly skilled riders and archers.

Real or Not?

"The image of a Centaur . . . is certainly not formed from the life, since no living creature of this sort ever existed." That was the firm opinion of the Roman philosopher Lucretius, who lived during the first century BCE. He continued:

Nor at any time can there be creatures of double nature and twofold body combined together of incompatible limbs, such that the powers of the two halves can be fairly balanced. Here is a proof that will convince the dullest wit. Firstly, the horse is at the best of his vigour when three years have passed round; not so the boy by any means. . . . Afterwards, when the strong powers of the horse are failing in old age and his body faints as life recedes, then is the time of the flower of boyhood, when youth is beginning.

One of the reasons Lucretius went to the trouble of explaining all this was that many people continued to believe centaurs really did exist, or that at least they had existed in a previous age. The Greek philosopher Empedocles, who lived during the fifth century BCE, had an evolutionary theory that accounted for creatures like centaurs. A later author explained: "Empedocles held that the first generations of animals and plants were not complete but consisted of separate limbs not joined together; the second, arising from the joining of these limbs, were like creatures in dreams; the third was the generation of whole-natured forms." The fourth generation included humans and other modern species. Meanwhile, though, many plants and animals of the older generations were unable to survive and went extinct.

But maybe they didn't *all* die out. There were plenty of people who thought it was possible a few of those beings "like creatures in dreams" were still around—beings such as centaurs. Pliny the Elder, in his multivolume *Natural History*, reported that the emperor Claudius "informs us, in his writings, that a Hippocentaur was born in Thessaly [a region of Greece], but died on the same day: and indeed I have seen one myself, which in the reign of that emperor was brought to him from Egypt, preserved in honey." This centaur was supposedly one of a herd of centaurs spotted in

Arabia. Its mummified, honey-soaked body remained on exhibit in the emperor's palace for many decades.

When the second-century Greek author Aelian considered centaurs, he thought it was natural to assume "that time produced these creatures by blending dissimilar bodies into one. But whether in fact they came into being and visited us at one and the same period, or whether rumour . . . fashioned them and by some miraculous combination fused the halves of horse and a man while endowing them with a single soul"—well, that was something no one would ever know for sure.

What was certain was that many people in the ancient world *wanted* to believe in centaurs, as well as in other fantastic creatures. It was the same desire for wonders that we often still feel today. The centaur sightings mentioned by Pliny were not much different, after all, from modern reports of Bigfoot or the Loch Ness monster.

The Gandharvas

Many scholars have debated the exact origin of the word *centaur*. One common explanation is that it meant "bull killer" or "bull hunter." The twentieth-century writer Jorge Luis Borges offered a different theory: "It has been said that the word 'Centaur' derives from 'gandharva'; in Vedic [ancient Indian] mythology, the Gandharva are minor deities who rule over the horses of the sun." When we remember that the *c* in *centaur* was originally pronounced like a *k*, it doesn't seem like such a far jump from *centaur* to *gandharva*. In any case, Gandharvas were often described as having the heads of men but the bodies of shaggy horses—although they could also take the form of handsome human warriors. They could indeed be warlike, but their main enemies were snake spirits called Nagas. Gandharvas were most often found in forests, mountainous places, and the air. They spent much of their time guarding the wine of the gods, teaching the healing arts to humans, and playing music. Their beautiful melodies accompanied the dances of the Apsarases, the heavenly maidens whom the Gandharvas loved.

Above: The king of the Gandharvas playing a lute, portrayed in a Tibetan painting from the 1600s.

THE FAMOUS AND THE INFAMOUS

Centaurs have beauty, maybe.

~OVID, FIRST CENTURY

MANY PEOPLE, IN ANCIENT TIMES AND ALL the centuries since, have not cared whether centaurs ever really existed. The myths had their own kind of truth and meaning—and they were usually interesting, exciting stories. Diodorus Siculus pondered the meaning of myths: "I am not unaware that many difficulties beset those who undertake to give an account of the ancient myths. . . . For some readers set up an unfair standard and require in the accounts of the myths the same exactness as in the events of our own time." That, however, was the wrong approach for understanding and enjoying mythology. With myths, "a man should by no means scrutinize the truth with so sharp an eye. In the theatres, for instance, though we are persuaded

Opposite: Chiron the centaur with his student Achilles, who would become one of Greece's most renowned warriors.

that there existed no Centaurs who are composed of two different kinds of bodies . . . we yet look with favour upon such products of the myths as these."

The Wise Centaur

To the ancient Greeks, centaurs generally symbolized the untamed forces of nature, and also the uncivilized ways of barbarians. The centaur Chiron, however, stood apart from all others of his kind. In the Greek poet Homer's epic the *Iliad*, Chiron is called "the most righteous of the Centaurs." His father was Cronus, who had taken the shape of a horse when he visited a beautiful daughter of Ocean, who became Chiron's mother. Cronus was a Titan, one of the ancient powers of the earth, and one of his other children was Zeus—so Chiron was a half brother of the king of the gods.

Chiron became famous for his supreme skills in hunting, music, medicine, and other fields of knowledge. As a result, many families wanted their sons to be educated by him. A number of the heroes of Greek legend were said to have been Chiron's students, including Jason and several of his shipmates. Later, Achilles and his close friend Patroclus were left with Chiron while their fathers went off adventuring with Jason. The two boys studied side by side, learning to ride, play the harp, and throw javelins. Thanks to Chiron's lessons, as men they would win lasting glory in the Trojan War.

Chiron's greatest pupil was Asclepius. He was the son of a mortal woman and Apollo, god of poetry and light. Asclepius mastered all of Chiron's vast knowledge of herbs and healing and eventually became fully divine as the god of medicine—"that craftsman of new health for weary limbs and banisher of pain," as Pindar called him.

Daughters and Death

Chiron and his wife had four daughters. One, called Ocyrhoe, had "learned prophetic singing." When she first saw young Asclepius, she was filled with the spirit of prophecy and proclaimed his fate. Prophecy continued to flow through her, and she told Chiron's future, too.

Unfortunately for Ocyrhoe, this was something the gods did not want known. As a result, they deprived her of speech, and even of humanity. These were her last words, according to the Roman poet Ovid:

> Human features
> Seem to be going from me. I am driven
> to canter over meadows, and for food
> Grass is my craving. Part of me, I know,
> Was always animal, but even so,
> My father, at least, was always
>   partly human.

In a few more moments, Ocyrhoe had been changed entirely into a horse, and there was nothing Chiron could do about it.

There was nothing he could do, either, about his own fate. He got caught in the middle of a battle between the other centaurs and Zeus's half-human son Heracles, who accidentally shot Chiron with a poisoned arrow. There was no antidote to the poison, which caused horrible pain—and since Chiron was immortal, he would suffer that agony forever. Heracles was desperate to help, so he persuaded Zeus to allow Chiron to die.

The gods preserved Chiron's image in the stars. This illustration of Sagittarius is from a twelfth-century English manuscript.

Zeus could not bear for the noble centaur to go to the underworld, however. Instead he placed him among the stars as the constellation Sagittarius.

A Centaur's Revenge

In the battle that led to Chiron's death, Heracles killed a large number of centaurs. The survivors fled, but eventually Heracles encountered one of them again. This centaur's name was Nessus.

For some time Nessus had been working as a kind of living ferry, carrying people on his back across a swift-flowing river. One day Heracles and his new wife, Deianira, came to the riverbank. Heracles was strong enough to swim across on his own, but he had to entrust his bride to the centaur. In the middle of the river, however, Nessus tried to run off with Deianira. She screamed, and Heracles heard her just as he reached the opposite bank. He immediately drew his bow and shot one of his poisoned arrows at Nessus.

As Heracles plunged back into the water to get Deianira, the centaur used his dying breath to take his revenge on the hero. Nessus told the young woman to catch some of the blood that was gushing out of his wound. He said it was a certain love potion, and told her how to use it if she ever suspected Heracles no longer loved her. For some reason, she actually believed Nessus.

Sure enough, a time came when Deianira thought her husband had fallen in love with someone else, and she was desperate to win him back. She had saved the centaur's blood and now she smeared it on a shirt, which she gave to her husband. The blood, however, had absorbed the poison from Heracles' arrow, and so he suffered the same agonies that Chiron had endured. Finally the hero's mor-

tal body died, and Zeus took the divine spirit that remained and made Heracles a god.

Centaurs Behaving Badly

Before his encounter with Nessus, according to some versions of the tale, Heracles took part in a great battle between the Lapiths and the centaurs. This was perhaps the most famous centaur story in Greek mythology and was a favorite subject for artists. It was a battle full of the drama of heroes fighting monsters, as Homer said in the *Iliad*: "These were the strongest generation of earth-born mortals, the strongest, and they fought against the strongest, the beast-men living within the mountains."

The trouble started when Pirithous, Ixion's son and successor as king of the Lapiths, invited all his relatives—including the centaurs—to his wedding. Of course he also invited all his friends, many of whom happened to be famous heroes. Foremost among them was Theseus, who had slain the Minotaur, a ferocious

The wedding of Perithous and Hippodameia turned ugly when one of the centaur guests tried to carry off the bride.

bull-headed man. At first everyone was getting along and having a good time at the wedding feast. Then, unfortunately, the centaurs got drunk, especially one named Eurytus—"His brain went wild with drinking, and in his fury he did much harm," Homer wrote in the *Odyssey*.

When Eurytus tried to carry off the bride, the other centaurs followed his example and seized the female wedding guests. Theseus was the first to react, shouting, in Ovid's words:

"What is this, Eurytus? Are you crazy?
To insult Pirithous while I live, to attack him
And so attack us both?" And the great hero,
By way of proving his words, pushed off the Centaurs,
Rescued the bride from all that raging fury.
Eurytus said nothing, there was nothing
For him to say; instead, he rushed at Theseus.

Enraged, Theseus grabbed a large, heavy wine bowl and threw it at Eurytus, killing him instantly. The other centaurs then attacked, and the battle was on. With fierce fighting, Theseus and the Lapiths slew many of the centaurs, and drove the rest out into the wilderness. This wasn't the end of the conflict, though. Marshaling their forces, the centaurs declared war on the Lapiths. With Theseus's help the Lapiths were victorious, but ever since then, as Homer wrote, "there has been a feud between men and Centaurs."

The Female Centaur and Her Love

Very few female centaurs were mentioned in ancient literature, but one of them, Hylonome, was made quite famous by the poet Ovid:

> Hylonome, of those half-beasts the fairest
> In all the woods . . .
> And she was dainty, if such creatures could be,
> Combing her hair, or mane, twining her locks
> With rosemary, or violets, or roses,
> Or sometimes with white lilies.

Hylonome was not only beautiful but also faithful and brave. In the battle with the Lapiths, she fought side by side with her beloved, the handsome young centaur Cyllarus. When he was struck by a spear and she could not save him, she threw herself onto the same spear blade so that the two of them could travel to the underworld together, companions in death as they had been in life.

Above: A rare image of a female centaur, from nineteenth-century Italy.

SATYRS, FAUNS, AND OTHERS

Goat-footed Pans will sing with the sighing reedpipe.

~PROPERTIUS, FIRST CENTURY BCE

ENTAURS WEREN'T THE ONLY BEAST-MEN running around Greek and Roman mythology. There was also a whole group of beings who were human above the waist and goats below. While centaurs, however, tended to be looked upon as enemies of civilization, the goat-people could be quite helpful. They were much honored by farmers and shepherds, who looked to them to protect the flocks and bring abundance to the fields and vineyards. You still had to watch out for the goat-legged beings, though. Since they were spirits of wild nature, their energies could sometimes become chaotic and destructive, just like any other force of nature.

SPIRITS OF FIELD AND FOREST

The community of ancient goat-people came to include satyrs, sileni, pans, fauns, and silvani. In early Greek art, the satyrs were

Opposite:
A watercolor painting from the early 1600s portrays a satyr who looks more like a troublemaker than like a peaceful guardian of fields and flocks.

depicted as men with the tails and pointed ears of horses. Gradually they became more and more goatlike, so that it was often difficult to tell the difference between them and other goat beings, especially since all these spirits behaved much the same way. They lived in woods, on hillsides, and near pastures. In general they were rowdy, mischievous, and loved wine, women, and song.* Not surprisingly, then, many of them were companions of the wine god Dionysus.

Sileni were elderly satyrs. Their leader was Silenus, usually pictured as a potbellied bald man. He had been one of Dionysus's tutors when the god was a child and then became one of his most faithful followers. It was said that Silenus was the one who suggested Dionysus invent wine, and Silenus tended to drink a lot of it himself. Luckily, it made him jolly, not violent as it did with the centaurs.

Pans were goat-men who took their name from Pan, a powerful and complex god. People who found themselves alone in a wild place sometimes felt an overwhelming terror at the strength of his spirit

A 1642 illustration of a music-loving satyr playing a long horn.

*Early on, all the goat-footed beings were male. Eventually, though, artists and writers started portraying female satyrs, pans, fauns, and silvani.

surrounding them—our word *panic* comes from his name. In general, though, he was a cheerful deity who was much loved by country people and poets. This devotion was expressed by an anonymous early Greek writer in a hymn:

> Tell me about Pan . . . with his goat's feet and two horns—a lover of merry noise. Through wooded glades he wanders . . . the shepherd-god, long-haired, unkempt. . . . Hither and thither he goes through the close thickets, now lured by soft streams, and now he presses on amongst towering crags and climbs up to the highest peak that overlooks the flocks. . . . Only at evening, as he returns from the chase, he sounds his note, playing sweet and low on his pipes of reed. . . . At that hour the clear-voiced nymphs are with him and move with nimble feet, singing . . . in a soft meadow where crocuses and sweet-smelling hyacinths bloom at random in the grass.

Surrounded by hyacinths and crocuses, Pan plays his pipes for an awestruck nymph.

The Romans sometimes referred to Pan by their own name for him, Faunus; the lesser spirits who were like him were then called fauns. The silvani were similar to the other goat beings. They, too, took after a god, Silvanus. Faunus and Silvanus (and therefore fauns and silvani) were sometimes confused with one another. The first was a god of hunting and farming, woods and fields; the second was concerned with woods, pastures, and gardens.

Herne the Hunter is a being who continues to fascinate authors, filmmakers, and artists, who have included him in a variety of works in recent decades, such as this 1991 drawing.

HORNED HUNTERS

While Pan had goat horns, a number of gods and spirits in lands north of Greece and Rome were portrayed with ram horns, bull horns, or antlers. For instance, a sculpture from first-century Gaul (modern France) shows a bearded man with the ears and antlers of a deer and labels him with the name Cernunnos, Gaulish for "Horned One." Similar beings appear in numerous other images from places where the Gauls and related peoples lived. In many of these depictions, the horned figure is accompanied by a stag. In one or two examples, he sits between a stag and a bull, and holds a bag from which coins are pouring out. These portrayals have been interpreted to mean that the horned deities were probably worshiped as gods of the hunt, herds, and abundance.

Such a being was still remembered in 1597, when William Shakespeare wrote:

There is an old tale goes that Herne the hunter,
Sometime a keeper here in Windsor Forest,
Doth all the winter time at still midnight
Walk round about an oak with great ragg'd horns.

Shakespeare added, however, that Herne was known to blast the oak, take livestock, and make cows give blood instead of milk—the horned spirit had changed from a protector of woods and herds to a destroyer of them. Yet the connection remained, and continued to fascinate people.

And we are still fascinated by human-animal hybrids. They have appeared in probably every art form ever produced, from cave paintings to computer games. They have meant different things to different people, from place to place and time to time. The meanings given to creatures like the sphinx and the centaur can tell us a lot about ourselves as human beings.

Most of all, we can see that these creatures matter to humanity, or they would not still be with us. Why do they matter? Perhaps they are a reminder of our connection to nature and to the other animals with whom we share the planet. Perhaps they also remind us of the strength that comes when reason and instinct work together. Perhaps, above all, they remind us of the power of the imagination.

GLOSSARY

amulet An object believed to give magical protection, good luck, or similar qualities to the person wearing or carrying it.

archaeologist A person who studies the tombs, ruins, art, everyday objects, and other remains of past societies.

barbarian To the ancient Greeks and Romans, someone who could not speak Greek or Latin and was therefore thought to be uncultured and uncivilized.

deity A goddess or god.

epic A long poem about the adventures of one or more legendary heroes.

myth A sacred story; a story about divine or semidivine beings.

mythology A body or collection of myths, such as the myths of a particular people.

nomad A member of a society based on herding animals and moving with them from one pasture to another throughout the year.

nymph An ancient Greek nature spirit pictured as a beautiful young woman.

scriptures Religious writings; holy books.

shaman A person who uses magical or divinely given powers to help his or her people by healing, ensuring plentiful game for hunting, communicating with the spirit world, and so on.

Trojan War A legendary ancient war in which Greek forces battled the city of Troy (in what is now western Turkey) for ten years.

TO LEARN MORE ABOUT SPHINXES AND CENTAURS

Books

Allen, Judy. *Fantasy Encyclopedia*. Boston: Kingfisher, 2005.

Curlee, Lynn. *Mythological Creatures: A Classical Bestiary*. New York: Atheneum Books for Young Readers, 2008.

Giblin, James Cross. *Secrets of the Sphinx*. New York: Scholastic Press, 2004.

Hile, Kevin. *Centaurs*. Detroit: Kidhaven Press, 2008.

Mortensen, Lori. *Sphinx*. Detroit: Kidhaven Press, 2008.

Websites

Atsma, Aaron J. *Theoi Greek Mythology: Bestiary*. www.theoi.com/Bestiary.html

British Museum. *Explore: Animals.*
    www.britishmuseum.org/explore/themes/animals/introduction.aspx

Jamieson, Cameron. "Assyrian Lamassu, Evil Repellent."
    www.assyriatimes.com/engine/modules/news/article.php?storyid=3199

Monstrous.com. *Mythological Monsters.*
    http://monsters.monstrous.com/index.htm

Winston, Allen. *The Great Sphinx of Giza, an Introduction.*
    www.touregypt.net/featurestories/sphinx1.html

Selected Bibliography

Allan, Tony. *The Mythic Bestiary: The Illustrated Guide to the World's Most Fantastical Creatures.* London: Duncan Baird, 2008.

Atsma, Aaron J. *Kentauroi Thessalioi.* Theoi Project 2000–2008. www.theoi.com/Georgikos/KentauroiThessalioi.html

Bonfante-Warren, Alexandra. *Mythical Beasts: Traditions and Tales of Favorite Fabled Creatures.* New York: MetroBooks, 2000.

Borges, Jorge Luis, with Margarita Guerrero. *The Book of Imaginary Beings.* Translated by Andrew Hurley. New York: Penguin Books, 2005.

Cherry, John, ed. *Mythical Beasts.* San Francisco: Pomegranate Artbooks, 1995.

Delacampagne, Ariane, and Christian Delacampagne. *Here Be Dragons: A Fantastic Bestiary.* Princeton, NJ: Princeton University Press, 2003.

duBois, Page. *Centaurs and Amazons: Women and the Pre-History of the Great Chain of Being.* Ann Arbor: University of Michigan Press, 1991.

Hamilton, Edith. *Mythology.* Boston: Little, Brown, 1942.

Mayor, Adrienne. *The First Fossil Hunters: Paleontology in Greek and Roman Times.* Princeton, NJ: Princeton University Press, 2000.

Nigg, Joseph. *The Book of Fabulous Beasts: A Treasury of Writings from Ancient Times to the Present.* New York: Oxford University Press, 1999.

Ovid. *Metamorphoses.* Translated by Rolfe Humphries. Bloomington: Indiana University Press, 1955.

Rose, Carol. *Giants, Monsters, and Dragons: An Encyclopedia of Folklore, Legend, and Myth.* New York: W. W. Norton, 2000.

Rosen, Brenda. *The Mythical Creatures Bible: The Definitive Guide to Legendary Beings.* New York: Sterling, 2009.

South, Malcolm, ed. *Mythical and Fabulous Creatures: A Sourcebook and Research Guide.* New York: Peter Bedrick Books, 1988.

Notes on Quotations

Chapter 1

p. 9 "Myriad kinds": Mayor, *The First Fossil Hunters*, p. 215.

p. 13 "a white animal": *Sahih Bukhari*, vol. 5, book 58, number 227, online at www.usc.edu/schools/college/crcc/engagement/resources/texts/muslim/hadith/bukhari/058.sbt.html

p. 13 "The animal's step": Ibid.

Chapter 2

p. 15 "In front of these pyramids": Cherry, *Mythical Beasts*, p. 106.

p. 17 "He relaxed in the shadow": Christine El Mahdy, *Tutankhamen: The Life and Death of the Boy-King* (New York: St. Martin's Press, 1999), p. 325.

p. 18 "to guard the gates": Delacampagne, *Here Be Dragons*, p. 90.

Chapter 3

p. 23 "Beasts of the mountains": *Heilbrunn Timeline of Art History*, www.metmuseum.org/toah/works-of-art/32.143.2

p. 24 "I built thereon": Ibid.

p. 26 "I am Pazuzu": Bonfante-Warren, *Mythical Beasts*, p. 24.

p. 26 "a scorpion-man": Nigg, *The Book of Fabulous Beasts*, p. 22.

p. 27 "Trembling terror they inspire": *The Epic of Gilgamesh*, tablet 9, online at www.ancienttexts.org/library/mesopotamian/gilgameshtab9.htm

p. 29 "Along with the face": Allan, *The Mythic Bestiary*, p. 176.

Chapter 4

p. 31 "Farther on we come to": Pausanias, *Description of Greece* 9.26.2, quoted at www.theoi.com/Ther/Sphinx.html

p. 33 "When the Sphinx bore down": Euripides, *The Phoenician Women*, translated by Elizabeth Wyckoff, in *Euripides V* (Chicago: University of Chicago Press, 1959), p. 74.

p. 33 "What being with one voice": Bonfante-Warren, *Mythical Beasts*, p. 56.

p. 33 "A human being": Ibid.

p. 34 "Uprose the merry Sphinx": South, *Mythical and Fabulous Creatures*, p. 186.

p. 34 "lovely hair, who": Borges, *The Book of Imaginary Beings*, p. 103.

p. 35 "they were wind-spirits": South, *Mythical and Fabulous Creatures*, p. 155.

p. 35 "They immediately all swoop": Ibid., p. 156.

p. 35 "No monster is more terrible": Ibid.

p. 35 "Famine shall fasten": Virgil, *The Aeneid*, translated by Cecil Day Lewis (New York: Doubleday, 1953), p. 67.

Chapter 5

p. 37 "He had indeed": Diodorus Siculus, *The Library of History* 4.12.3, quoted at www.theoi.com/Georgikos/KentaurosPholos.html

p. 37 "a wild folk": Strabo, *Geography* 9.5.19, quoted at Atsma, *Kentauroi Thessalioi*.

p. 38 "her babe of monstrous": Pindar, *Pythian Ode* 2, quoted at Atsma, *Kentauroi Thessalioi*.

p. 38 "And she reared him": South, *Mythical and Fabulous Creatures*, p. 230.

p. 38 "used to think": Philostratus the Elder, *Imagines* 2.3, quoted at Atsma, *Kentauroi Thessalioi*.

p. 39 "Who [in this day and age]": Cicero, *De Natura Deorum* 2.2., quoted at Atsma, *Kentauroi Thessalioi*.

p. 39 "because they were the first": Diodorus Siculus, *The Library of History* 4.69.4, quoted at Atsma, *Kentauroi Thessalioi*.

p. 40 "The image of a Centaur": Nigg, *The Book of Fabulous Beasts*, p. 50.

p. 41 "Nor at any time": Borges, *The Book of Imaginary Beings*, p. 47.

p. 41 "Empedocles held that": duBois, *Centaurs and Amazons*, p. 69.

p. 41 "informs us, in his writings": Pliny the Elder, *The Natural History* 7.3, translated by John Bostock, online at www.perseus.tufts.edu/hopper/collections

p. 42 "that time produced": Aelian, *On Animals* 17.9, quoted at Atsma, *Kentauroi Thessalioi*.

p. 43 "It has been said": Borges, *The Book of Imaginary Beings*, p. 45.

Chapter 6

p. 45 "Centaurs have beauty": Ovid, *Metamorphoses*, p. 297.

p. 45 "I am not unaware" and "a man should": Diodorus Siculus, *The Library of History* 4.8.1-4, translated by C. H. Oldfather, online at http://penelope.uchicago.edu/Thayer/E/Roman/Texts/Diodorus_Siculus/4B*.html

p. 46 "the most righteous": South, *Mythical and Fabulous Creatures*, p. 227.

p. 46 "that craftsman of new health": Pindar, *Pythian Ode* 3, quoted at www.theoi.com/Georgikos/KentaurosKheiron.html

p. 47 "learned prophetic singing": Ovid, *Metamorphoses*, p. 48.

p. 47 "Human features": Ibid., p. 49.

p. 49 "These were the strongest": Homer, *Iliad*, 1.266–268, translated by Richmond Lattimore, online at www.library.northwestern.edu/homer/html/application.html

p. 50 "His brain went wild": South, *Mythical and Fabulous Creatures*, p. 228.

p. 50 "What is this, Eurytus?": Ovid, *Metamorphoses*, p. 292.

p. 50 "there has been a feud": South, *Mythical and Fabulous Creatures*, p. 228.

p. 51 "Hylonome, of those half-beasts": Ovid, *Metamorphoses*, p. 297.

Chapter 7

p. 53 "Goat-footed Pans": Propertius, *Elegies* 3.17, online at www.thelatinlibrary.com/prop3.html#17 (translation by Kathryn Hinds).

p. 55 "Tell me about Pan": "Hymn 19 to Pan," *The Homeric Hymns*, translated by Hugh G. Evelyn-White, online at www.perseus.tufts.edu/hopper/collections

p. 56 "There is an old tale": *The Merry Wives of Windsor*, act 4, scene 4, in William Shakespeare, *The Complete Works: Compact Edition*, edited by Stanley Wells and others (Oxford: Clarendon Press, 1988), p. 503.

Index

ABOUT THE AUTHOR

KATHRYN HINDS grew up near Rochester, New York. She studied music and writing at Barnard College, and went on to do graduate work in comparative literature and medieval studies at the City University of New York. She has written more than forty books for young people, including *Everyday Life in the Roman Empire*, *Everyday Life in the Renaissance*, *Everyday Life in Medieval Europe*, and the books in the series BARBARIANS, LIFE IN THE MEDIEVAL MUSLIM WORLD, LIFE IN ELIZABETHAN ENGLAND, and LIFE IN ANCIENT EGYPT. Kathryn lives in the north Georgia mountains with her husband, their son, and two cats. When she is not reading or writing, she enjoys dancing, gardening, knitting, and taking walks in the woods. Visit Kathryn online at www.kathrynhinds.com